Usborne Beginners

Horses and ponies

Anna Milbourne

Designed by Josephine Thompson

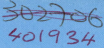
302706
401934

FALKIRK COUNCIL
LIBRARY SUPPORT
FOR SCHOOLS

302706

This book is to be returned on or before
the last date stamped below.

PROJECTS

D0302057

Library Services
Victoria Buildings
Queen Street
Falkirk
FK2 7AF

636
1

Falkirk Council

Contents

Wild horses

In the wild, horses and ponies live in groups called herds.

This is a herd of wild ponies. Ponies are small horses.

Life in a herd

Horses like to live in
a herd because it
feels safer than
living on their own.

Some wild animals kill horses. In a herd of
horses, some keep watch while others eat.

If one of the horses sees danger, it runs
away. The others copy it and run away too.

A herd of wild horses usually has lots of female horses, called mares.

One mare is bossier than all the others. She leads the herd. A herd usually has one male horse, called a stallion. He runs at the back.

Horses and ponies don't like living on their own.

Coats and tails

Horses have hair all over their bodies. This is called a coat.

Their coats can be plain or patterned.

Horses with this pattern are called Pinto or Paint horses.

All horses have long tails.

In summer, a horse swishes its tail to brush away flies.

In winter, a horse's tail helps to keep its bottom warm.

Horses' coats grow
long and bushy
in the winter.
This keeps
them warm.

Many horses
and ponies like to
live outside all year
round, even in the
cold snow.

Horses' coats often change as they grow up.

Running

Horses are very, very good at running. Their long legs help them to run fast. In the wild, this helps them to escape from danger.

When horses run fast, it's called galloping.

When they run slowly, it's called cantering.

The first thing a horse does if it's scared, is run.

When they jog, it's called trotting.

When they walk, it's just called walking.

Foals

Baby horses are called foals. A foal learns how to walk in the first hour of its life.

When a foal is born, its mother licks it clean.

The foal tries to stand up but keeps falling over.

It learns to stand, then takes its first few wobbly steps.

A few hours after a foal is born, it can run fast enough to keep up with a herd.

A new foal doesn't eat grass at first. It drinks its mother's milk from teats on her tummy.

This foal is drinking its mother's milk. It is one hour old.

Growing up

Young foals stay close to their mother at first.

As they get older, they play with other foals.

They like to kick in the air and run.

Male foals are called colts and female foals are called fillies.

Later, foals start to eat grass. They stop drinking their mother's milk.

Their legs are so long they can only just reach the grass at first.

Grown-up horses teach younger ones how to behave.

A young horse kicks a mare. She chases it to the edge of the herd.

It doesn't like being sent away. If it is good, it is allowed back.

13

Horse talk

You can tell how a horse feels by the way it looks and acts.

Horses lift up their top lip like this when they can smell or taste something interesting.

As well as using silent signals, horses neigh, snort and squeal.

A scared horse turns its ears back and shows the white parts of its eyes.

If a horse scrapes the ground with its hoof, it may be feeling impatient.

An excited horse will prance around holding its tail high in the air.

An angry horse flattens its ears all the way back and might show its teeth.

Keeping clean

When horses and ponies clean themselves, it is called grooming. They nibble their coats to get rid of dirt and bugs.

These horses are grooming each other. This shows they are friends.

This horse is rolling to scratch its back. Rolling rubs itchy insects off its coat, too.

People who keep pet horses groom them often. Most horses love being groomed.

First of all, the owner scrapes mud out of the horse's hooves.

She brushes its coat. Then, she brushes its mane and tail.

Trusting people

Wild horses are afraid of people. By copying how horses act with each other, a trainer can teach a horse not to be afraid.

If a horse wants to let another horse come near, it will turn away. It won't stare at the other horse.

To ask a horse to come, a trainer turns away, too. To the horse, this means, "Come to me. I won't hurt you."

Horses get to know people by how they smell.

Wild horses don't like being touched by people. They have to learn to trust them first.

Pet horses trust people and like being stroked.

Training horses

All horses act like wild horses until they are trained. Pet horses are trained from when they are born to get them ready for riding.

A trainer strokes a foal to help it get used to people.

Its mother stays close by to help it feel safe.

A foal learns how to be led around wearing a halter.

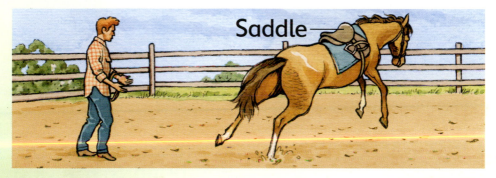

A young horse learns to wear a saddle. It feels strange at first, so the horse jumps around.

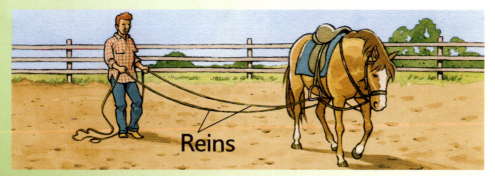

It is taught on long reins. It learns to turn left or right when the trainer moves the reins.

Life in a stable

Many pet horses live in stables with other horses and ponies.

They live near each other so they don't get lonely.

Every day, people clean out the stables and bring them food.

People come to the stables to ride or for riding lessons.

There is a field close by where the horses can run free.

Pet horses
wear metal
shoes so their
hooves don't
wear down.

This man is a farrier.
He is trimming the horse's
hoof before putting on a new shoe.

Horses get new shoes six to eight times a year.

Learning to ride

Lots of people ride horses for fun. It takes years to learn how to ride well.

This girl is jumping her pony over a log. You have to be a fairly good rider to do this.

24

Most horses and ponies are at least three years old before people ride them.

You can learn how to ride at a riding school.

1. At first, you learn how to get on and off a pony's back.

2. You learn to sit in the saddle without wobbling.

3. Next, you learn how to ask the pony to go, stop and turn.

4. Later, you learn how to trot and then canter on the pony.

Working horses

People use horses to help them work
and for sports.

Yakut ponies
live near the North Pole and
help people pull sleighs. It's so cold there
that no other kind of horse could survive.

Some horses work in the movies. They are
taught tricks, such as how to sit or fall over.

Thoroughbreds are a kind
of horse that can run very fast.
Most racehorses are thoroughbreds.

Police horses help to control crowds. They
have to be brave and calm to do their job.

They are trained not
to run away from
loud noises.

They learn to stay
calm with people
crowding around.

Horse power

Before engines were invented, horses were needed for carrying people and pulling things.

Instead of using tractors, farmers used powerful horses to help farm their fields.

The first trains were pulled along tracks by horses.

Strong horses pulled boats called barges along canals.

They ate out of nosebags as they walked along.

Before people had cars, they rode around in carriages pulled by horses.

Carriages like this one are still used on special occasions.

Glossary of horse words

Here are some of the words in this book you might not know. This page tells you what they mean.

 herd - a group of animals that live together like a family.

 foal - a baby horse or pony. A female foal is a filly and a male is a colt.

 teat - lots of female animals have teats. Their babies suck them to drink milk.

 grooming - when a person cleans a horse or when horses clean themselves.

 trainer - somebody who teaches or trains horses and ponies.

 stable - a place where pet horses and ponies live.

 farrier - a person who makes and fits horses' shoes.

Websites to visit

If you have a computer, you can find out more about horses and ponies on the Internet. On the Usborne Quicklinks website there are links to four fun websites.

Website 1 - Play a horse game.

Website 2 - Listen to some horse sounds.

Website 3 - Print out pictures of horses to fill in.

Website 4 - Find out more about horses and ponies.

To visit these websites, go to **www.usborne-quicklinks.com** and type the keywords "beginners horses". Then, click on the link for the website you want to visit. Before you use the Internet, look at the safety guidelines inside the back cover of this book and ask an adult to read them with you.

Index

Acknowledgements

Photographic manipulation: John Russell

The publishers are grateful to the following for permission to reproduce material:
© **Alamy Images**: 4-5 (Mark J. Barrett), 8-9 (Photovalley/MICEK); © **Ardea London**: 14
(M. Watson); © **Bob Langrish**: 7, 12, 28; © **Corbis**: cover (Tom Brakefield), 16 (Gunter Marx), 29
(Tim Graham); © **Getty**: 27 (Daikusan); © **Horsepix**: title page, 6, 13, 20, 31; © **ImageState**:
2-3; © **NHPA**: 26 (B&C Alexander); © **Powerstock**: 17 (Georgie Holland); © **Warren Photographic**: 11.
Photograph on page 24 by Kit Houghton.

Every effort has been made to trace and acknowledge ownership of copyright. If any rights have
been omitted, the publishers offer to rectify this in any subsequent editions following notification.

First published in 2004 by Usborne Publishing Ltd., Usborne House, 83-85 Saffron Hill, London EC1N 8RT,
England. www.usborne.com Copyright © 2004 Usborne Publishing Ltd. The name Usborne and the devices ♀ ◉
are Trade Marks of Usborne Publishing Ltd. All rights reserved. No part of this publication may be reproduced,
stored in a retrieval system, or transmitted in any form or by any means, electronic, mechanical,
photocopying, recording or otherwise without the prior permission of the publisher.
First published in America 2004. U.E. Printed in Belgium.